# THE BIG BOOK OF
# THINGS THAT GO

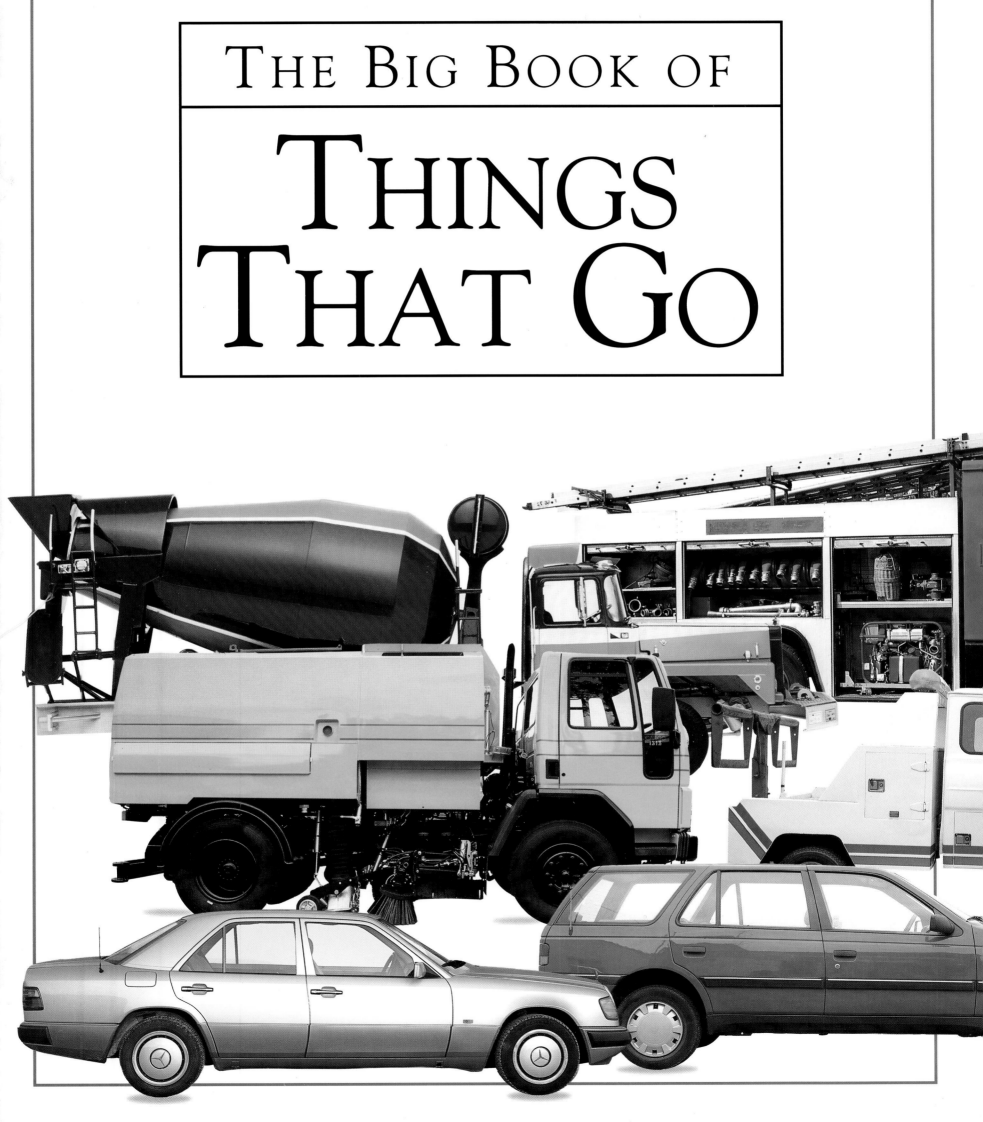

# A DK PUBLISHING BOOK

**Project Editor** Caroline Bingham
**Art Editor** Sara Hill
**U.S. Assistant Editor** Camela Decaire

**Senior Editor** Sheila Hanly
**Additional Design** Helen Melville
**Production** Josie Alabaster
**Picture Researcher** Joanna Thomas

**Photography by** Richard Leeney
**Additional Photography by** Lynton Gardner,
Finbar Hawkins, and Alex Wilson
**Illustrations by** Jonathan Heale

First American Edition, 1994
13 15 17 19 20 18 16 14 12

Published in the United States by
DK Publishing, Inc., 95 Madison Avenue
New York, NY 10016

Copyright © 1994 Dorling Kindersley Limited, London

Visit us on the World Wide Web at
http://www.dk.com

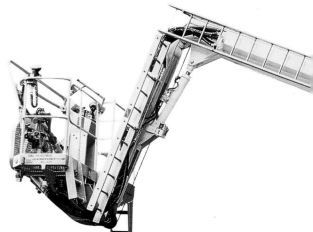

**Library of Congress Cataloging-in-Publication Data**
The Big book of things that go.—1st American ed.
p.   cm.
Includes index
ISBN 1-56458-462-3
1. Motor vehicles—Juvenile literature. [1. Motor vehicles.]
I. Dorling Kindersley Limited.
TL147.B54  1994
629.04'6—dc20                                          94-643
                                                        CIP
                                                        AC
Color reproduction by Chromagraphics, Singapore
Printed in Spain by Artes Gráficas Toledo, S.A.U.
D.L.TO: 141-1999

# THE BIG BOOK OF
# THINGS THAT GO

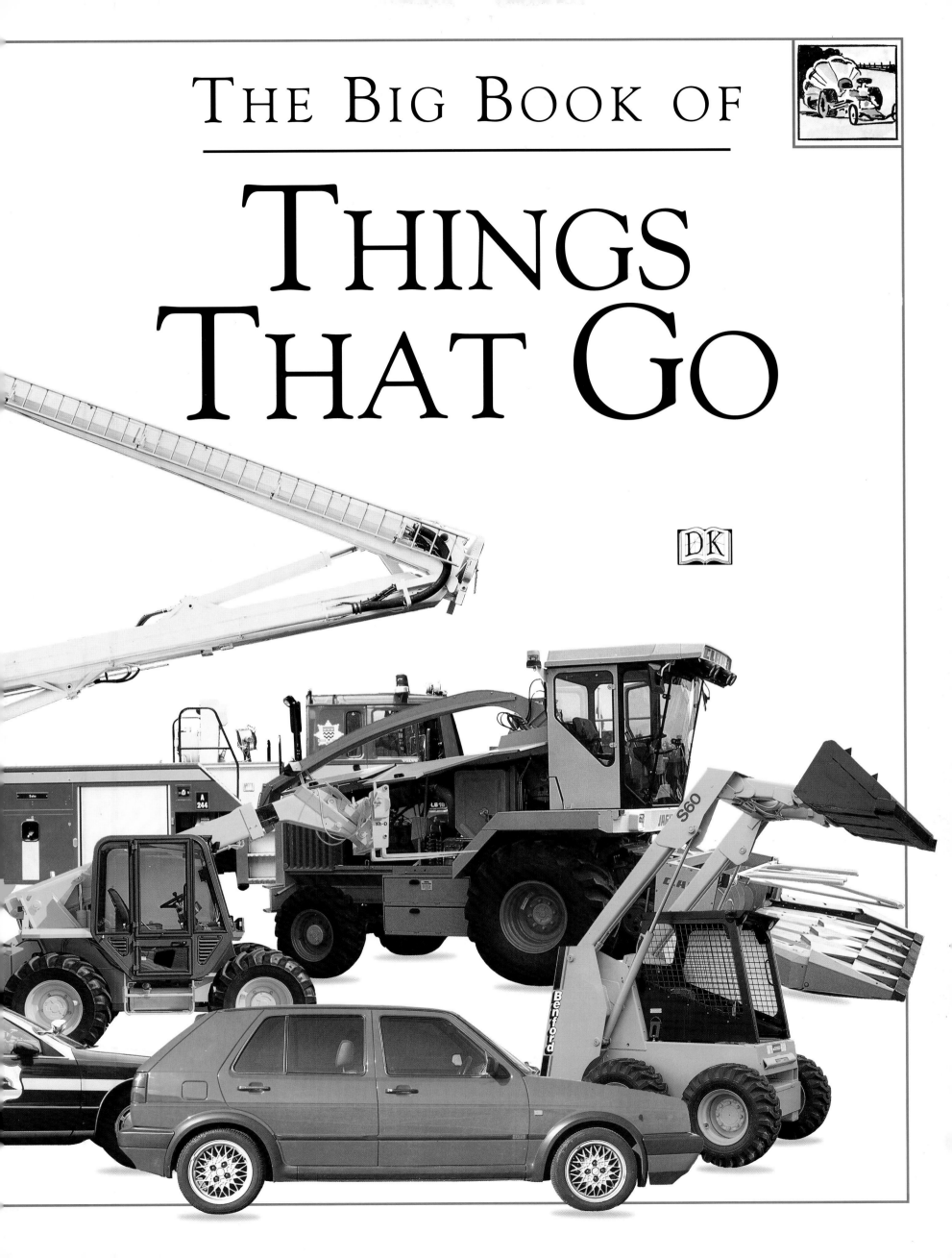

Truck loader crane
(page 23)

Delivery van
(page 8)

Articulated dump truck
(page 22)

Sports car
(page 6)

Roller
(page 21)

Giant dump truck
(page 31)

Racing motorcycle
(page 29)

Taxi
(page 9)

Coach
(page 6)

# Contents

On the road . . . . . . . . . . . . . . . . . . . . 6

In the city . . . . . . . . . . . . . . . . . . . . 8

On rails . . . . . . . . . . . . . . . . . . . . 10

At sea . . . . . . . . . . . . . . . . . . . . 12

On the water . . . . . . . . . . . . . . . . . . 14

In the air . . . . . . . . . . . . . . . . . . . . 16

On the farm . . . . . . . . . . . . . . . . . . 18

At the roadworks . . . . . . . . . . . . . . . 20

On the building site . . . . . . . . . . . . 22

Emergency! . . . . . . . . . . . . . . . . . 24

Firefighters . . . . . . . . . . . . . . . . . 26

At the races . . . . . . . . . . . . . . . . . 28

Amazing machines . . . . . . . . . . . . . 30

Index . . . . . . . . . . . . . . . . . . . 32

Hot-air
balloon
(page 17)

Sailboat
(page 14)

Race car
(page 28)

Go-cart
(page 28)

## Car carrier

This car carrier is taking new cars from a factory to be sold. How many cars do you count?

handlebars

## Camper van

Some people go on vacation in camper vans. Inside there are beds, a kitchen, and even a toilet.

## Motorcycle

Motorcycles have two wheels. The rider steers with handlebars.

## Sports car

A sports car's powerful engine and long, low shape help it zoom along at top speed.

engine

There is space under the hood for luggage.

## Coach

Coaches carry people on long journeys. This coach has a special place for baggage, and rows of comfortable seats.

Baggage is stored in these lockers.

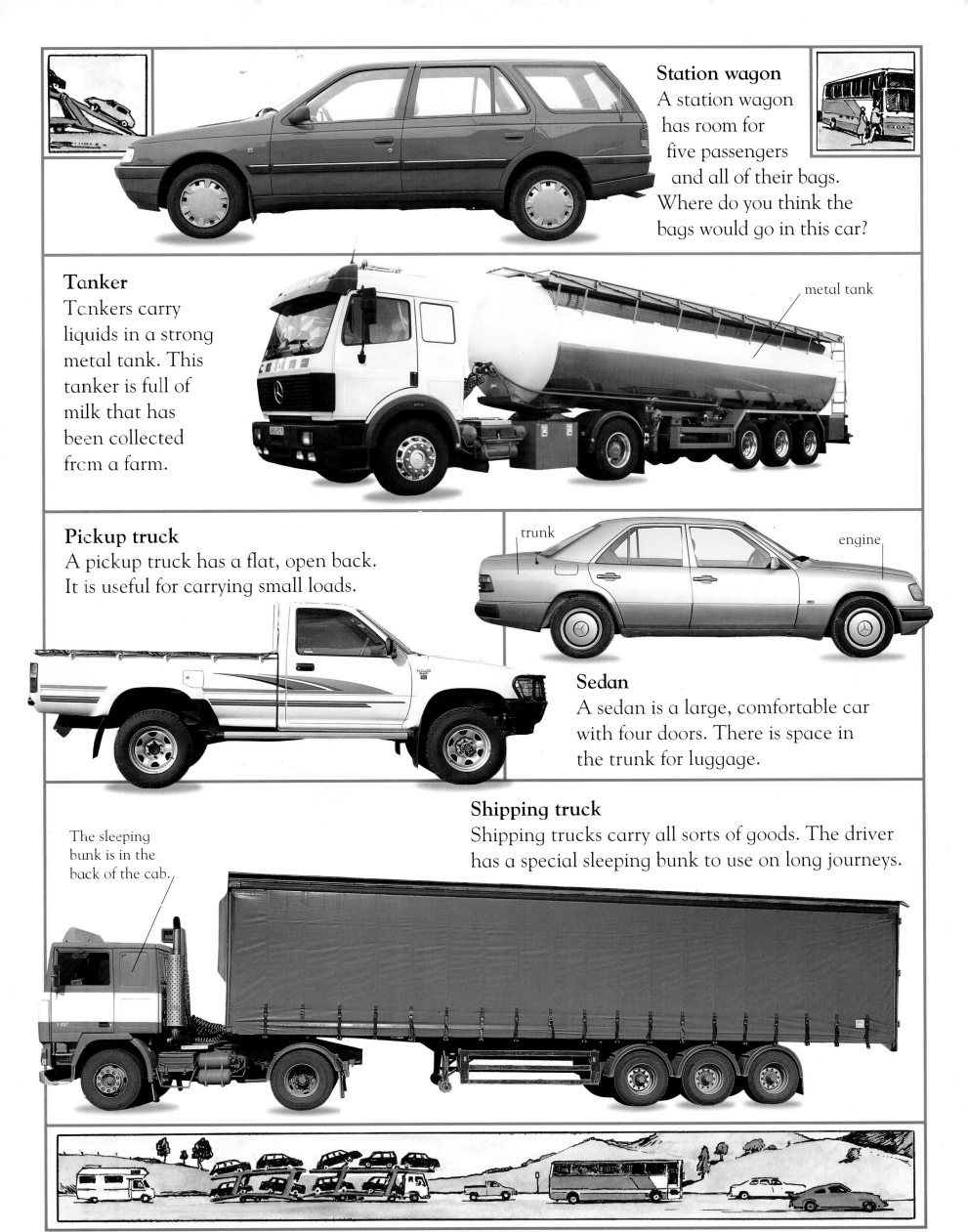

## Station wagon

A station wagon has room for five passengers and all of their bags. Where do you think the bags would go in this car?

## Tanker

Tankers carry liquids in a strong metal tank. This tanker is full of milk that has been collected from a farm.

metal tank

## Pickup truck

A pickup truck has a flat, open back. It is useful for carrying small loads.

trunk

engine

## Sedan

A sedan is a large, comfortable car with four doors. There is space in the trunk for luggage.

## Shipping truck

Shipping trucks carry all sorts of goods. The driver has a special sleeping bunk to use on long journeys.

The sleeping bunk is in the back of the cab.

# In the city

back door

### Hatchback

This hatchback has five doors. Can you find the fifth door? Hatchbacks are popular cars in cities because they are small and easy to park.

### Delivery van

Delivery vans carry goods to stores and people's homes. A sliding side door makes it easy to load up the back of a van.

side door

### Bus

People ride buses to go to school and work. A bus collects its passengers at a bus stop.

### Garbage truck

Garbage is often collected in trucks like this one. Bags of garbage are crunched up in the back of the truck.

### Bicycle

Riding a bicycle is a fast way to get around in a city. Have you ever ridden a bicycle?

seat

pedal

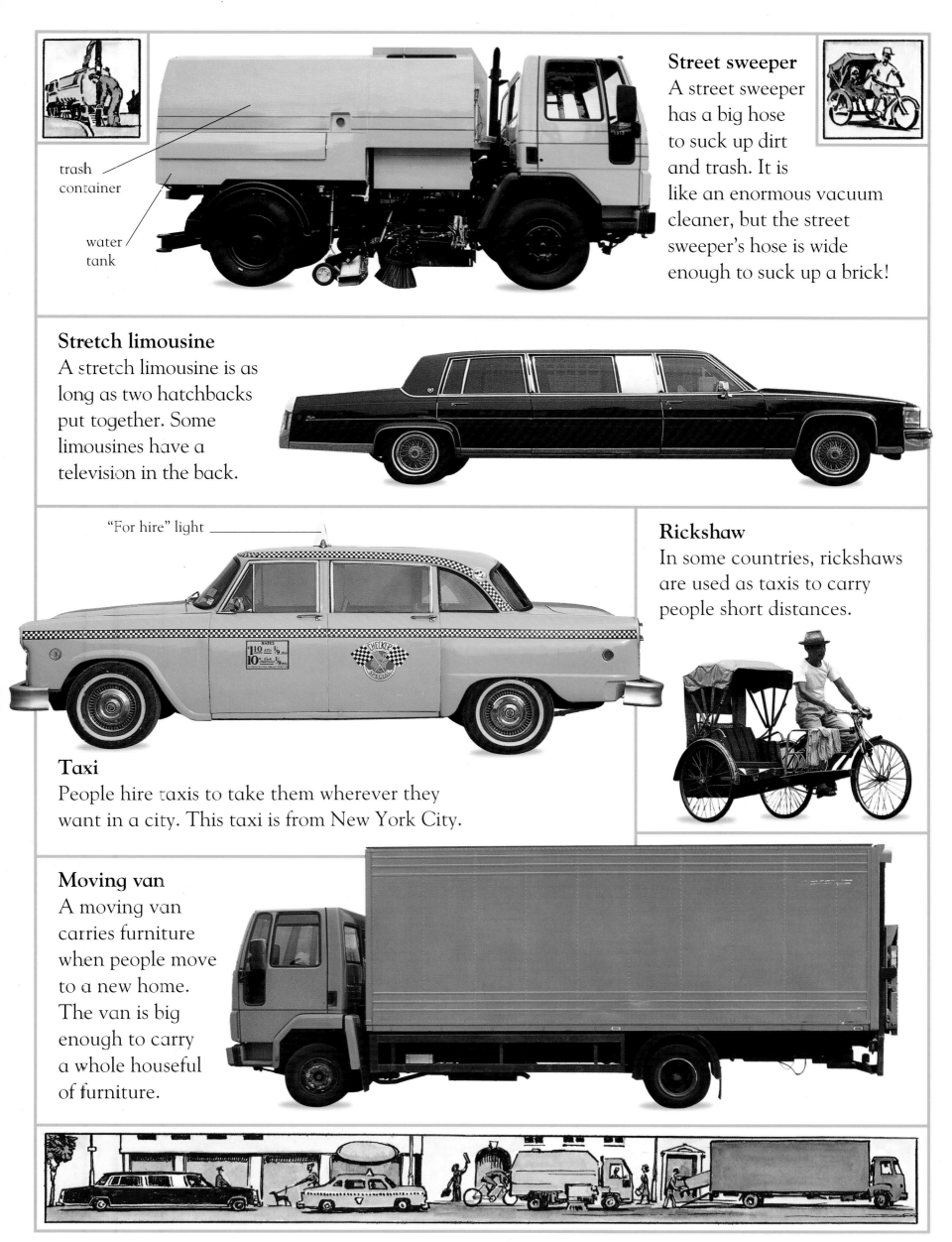

**Street sweeper**
A street sweeper has a big hose to suck up dirt and trash. It is like an enormous vacuum cleaner, but the street sweeper's hose is wide enough to suck up a brick!

trash container

water tank

**Stretch limousine**
A stretch limousine is as long as two hatchbacks put together. Some limousines have a television in the back.

"For hire" light

**Rickshaw**
In some countries, rickshaws are used as taxis to carry people short distances.

**Taxi**
People hire taxis to take them wherever they want in a city. This taxi is from New York City.

**Moving van**
A moving van carries furniture when people move to a new home. The van is big enough to carry a whole houseful of furniture.

9

# On rails

## Steam train

Trains are pulled by engines. A steam-engine driver shovels coal into a fire that heats water. The hot water turns into steam, which makes the engine go.

This car, called a tender, is full of coal and water.

## Diesel locomotive

This engine is very strong. It usually pulls up to 12 train cars along the rails.

engine

60082

## Streetcar

Streetcars are like buses, but they run on rails along city streets.

800

## Snowplow train

A snowplow train uses large propellers to blow snow off the rails.

## Monorail

Monorails run on one rail. They are used to carry people short distances.

### Subway train

A subway train speeds along tunnels built deep under a city's streets.

### Rack-and-pinion train

A rack-and-pinion train can travel up and down steep hills. It has a toothy wheel that slots into a special rail, like a cog in a machine.

conductor's cab

D26

### Shunter

A shunter pushes train cars and wagons around a railway yard. It needs a powerful engine.

These buffers are used to push the train cars.

### High-speed train

The French high-speed train, the TGV, is the fastest passenger train in the world. The train runs on electricity it picks up from overhead cables through a pantograph.

pantograph

TGV

TGVs usually travel on special tracks.

The train is controlled from this cab.

CRANE RUNNER

### Breakdown train

A breakdown train carries a giant crane. If a train car goes off the rails, the crane lifts it back into position.

# At sea

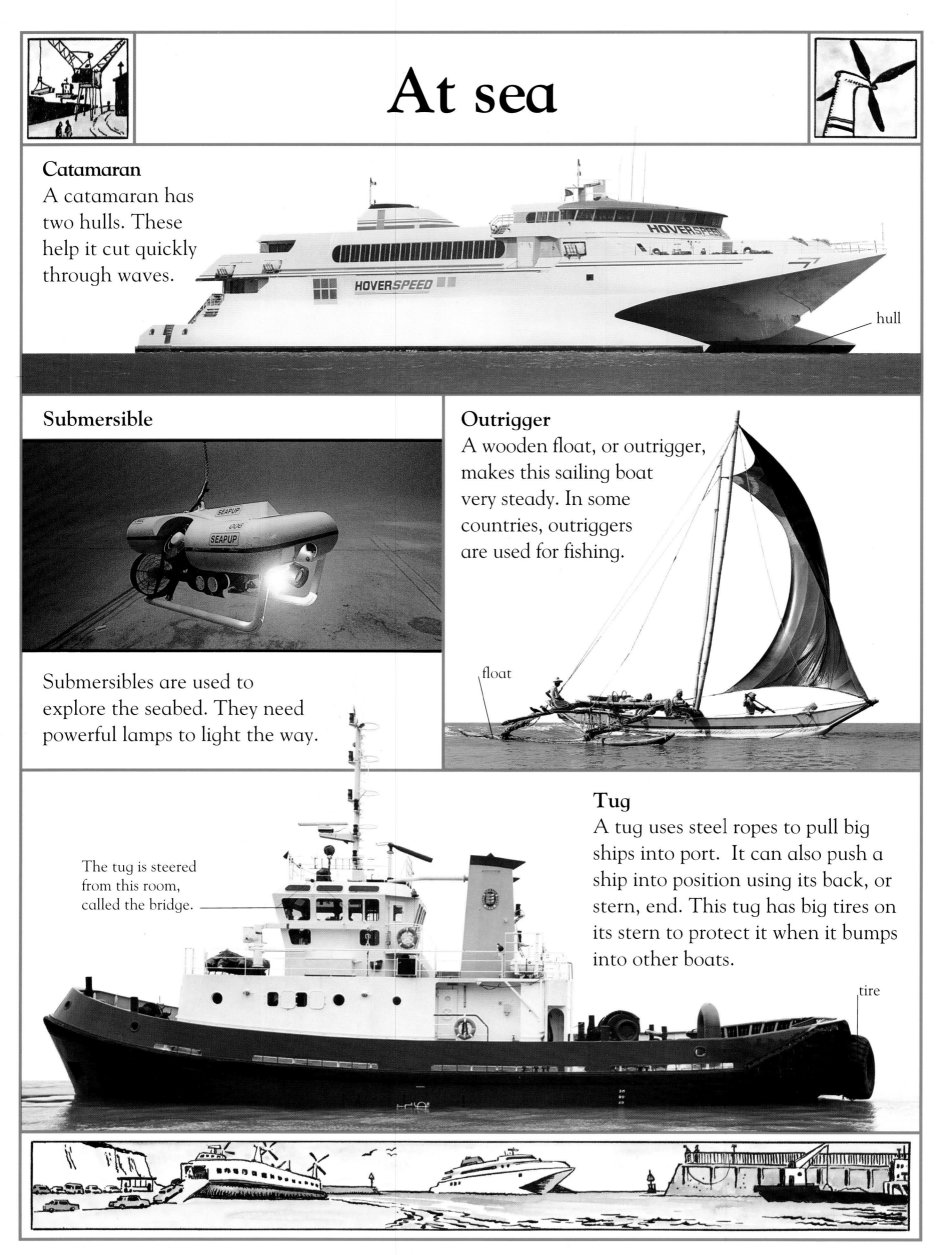

## Catamaran

A catamaran has two hulls. These help it cut quickly through waves.

hull

## Submersible

Submersibles are used to explore the seabed. They need powerful lamps to light the way.

## Outrigger

A wooden float, or outrigger, makes this sailing boat very steady. In some countries, outriggers are used for fishing.

float

## Tug

A tug uses steel ropes to pull big ships into port.  It can also push a ship into position using its back, or stern, end. This tug has big tires on its stern to protect it when it bumps into other boats.

The tug is steered from this room, called the bridge.

tire

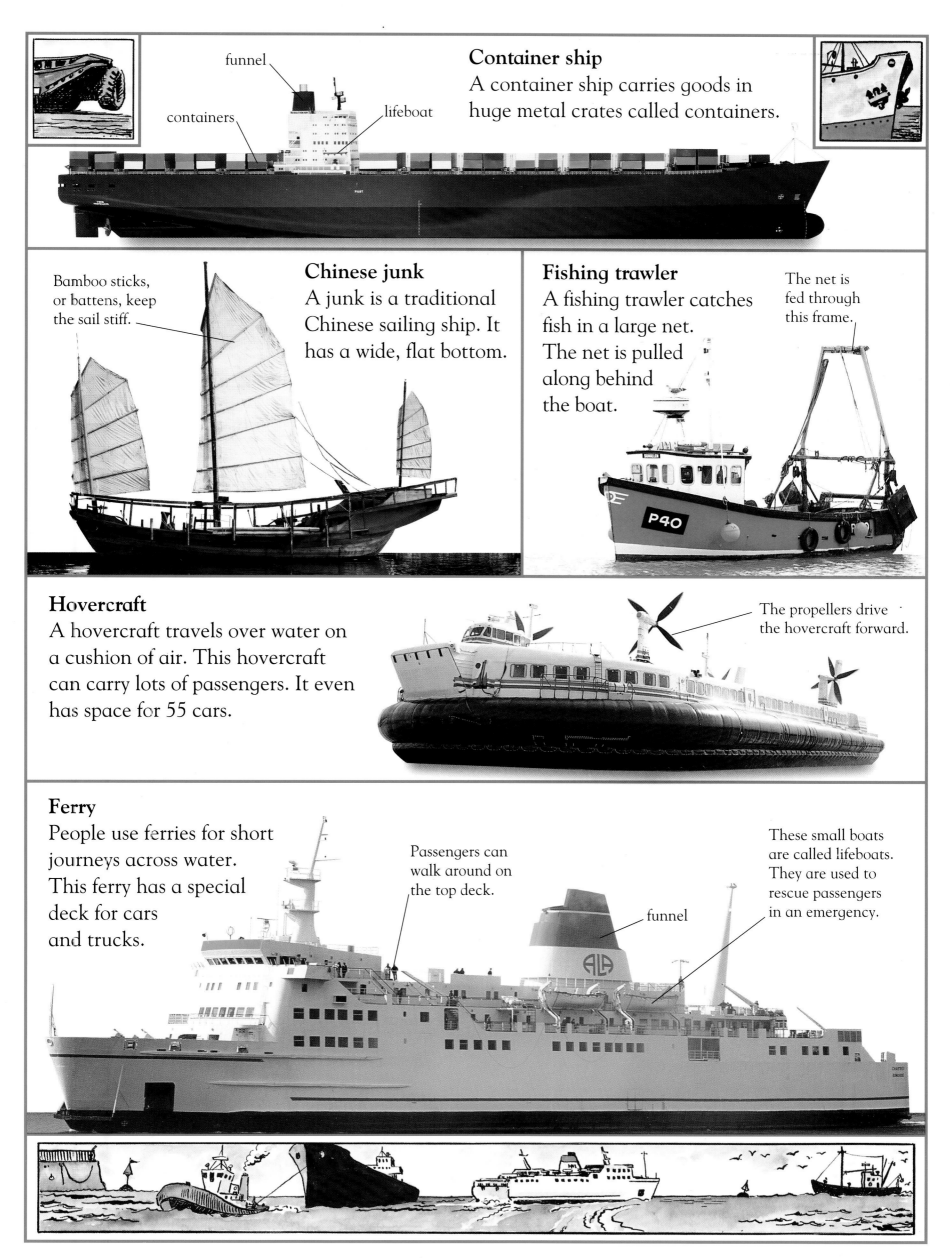

## Container ship

A container ship carries goods in huge metal crates called containers.

funnel

containers

lifeboat

## Chinese junk

A junk is a traditional Chinese sailing ship. It has a wide, flat bottom.

Bamboo sticks, or battens, keep the sail stiff.

## Fishing trawler

A fishing trawler catches fish in a large net. The net is pulled along behind the boat.

The net is fed through this frame.

P40

## Hovercraft

A hovercraft travels over water on a cushion of air. This hovercraft can carry lots of passengers. It even has space for 55 cars.

The propellers drive the hovercraft forward.

## Ferry

People use ferries for short journeys across water. This ferry has a special deck for cars and trucks.

Passengers can walk around on the top deck.

These small boats are called lifeboats. They are used to rescue passengers in an emergency.

funnel

13

# On the water

handlebars

**Sailboat**
This small sailboat can be sailed by only one or two people.

mast

mainsail

**Jet ski**
A jet ski is a lot like a water motorcycle. It whizzes over water at great speeds, bouncing over waves. The rider steers the jet ski with handlebars.

**Paddle steamer**
Paddle steamers like this one carry people on river trips. The huge paddle wheel turns in the water, pushing the boat forward.

paddle wheel

**Cabin cruiser**
Many people go on vacation in cabin cruisers. On board, there is space for them to cook and sleep.

life buoy

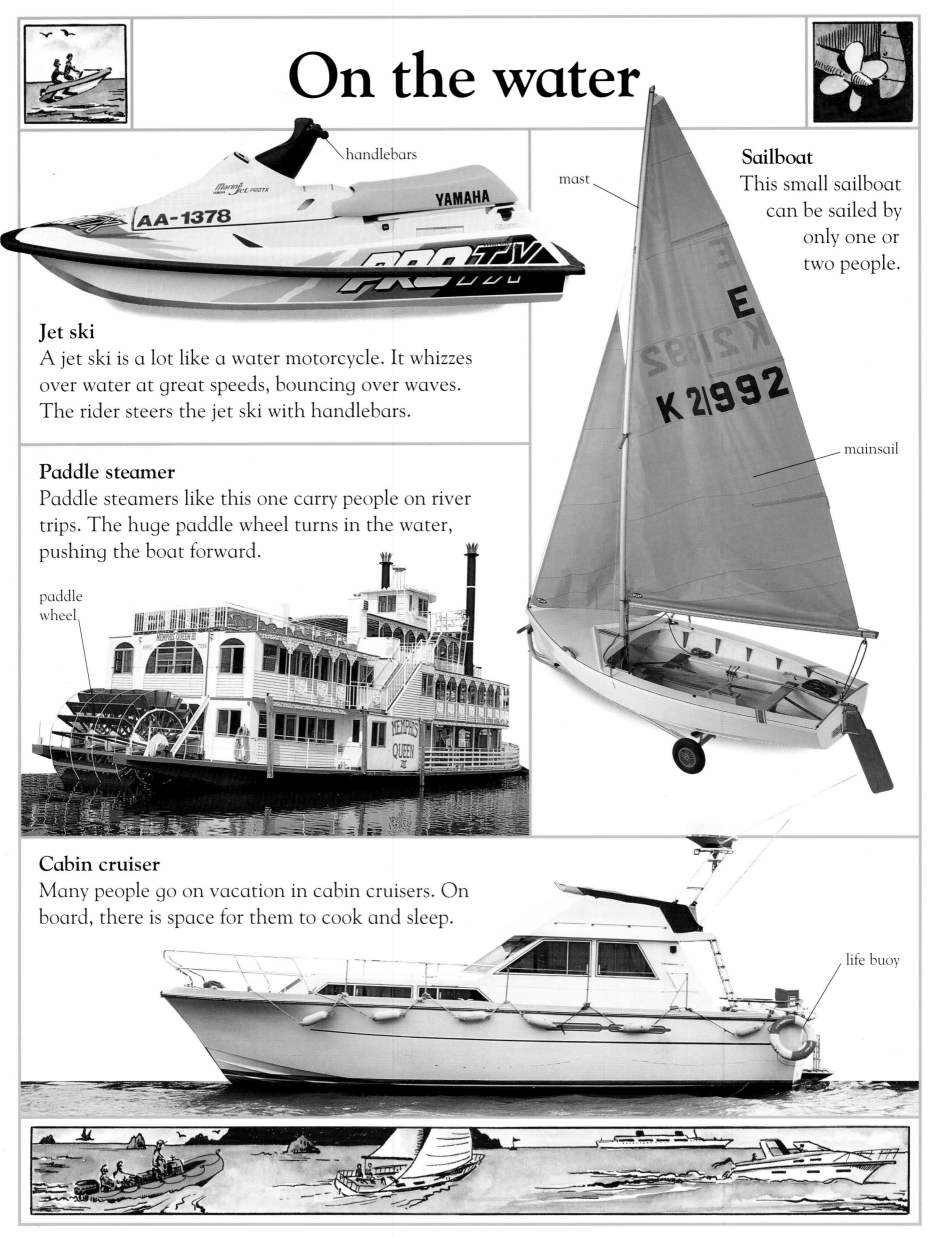

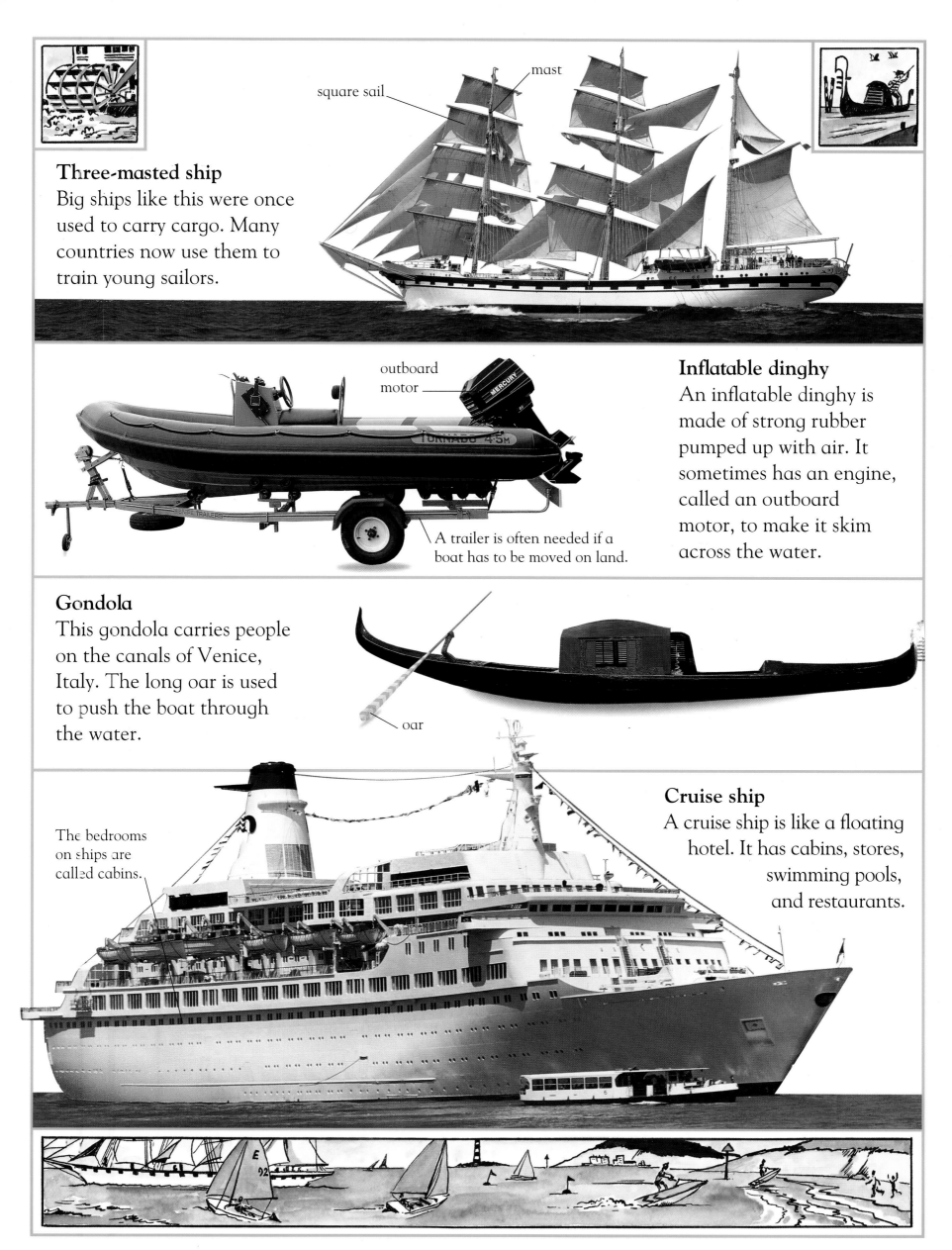

### Three-masted ship
Big ships like this were once used to carry cargo. Many countries now use them to train young sailors.

square sail

mast

### Inflatable dinghy
An inflatable dinghy is made of strong rubber pumped up with air. It sometimes has an engine, called an outboard motor, to make it skim across the water.

outboard motor

A trailer is often needed if a boat has to be moved on land.

### Gondola
This gondola carries people on the canals of Venice, Italy. The long oar is used to push the boat through the water.

oar

### Cruise ship
A cruise ship is like a floating hotel. It has cabins, stores, swimming pools, and restaurants.

The bedrooms on ships are called cabins.

# In the air

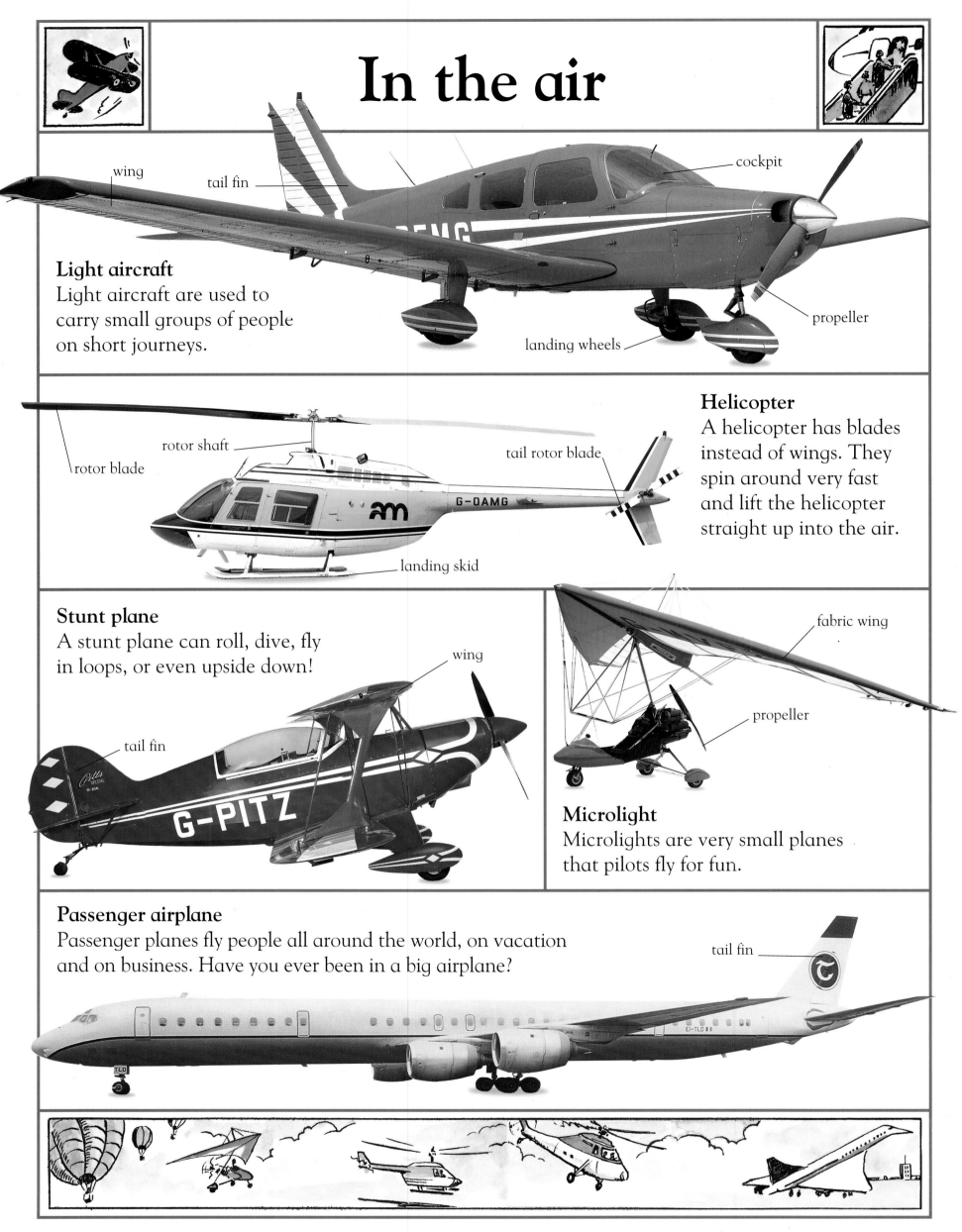

### Light aircraft
Light aircraft are used to carry small groups of people on short journeys.

wing

tail fin

cockpit

propeller

landing wheels

### Helicopter
A helicopter has blades instead of wings. They spin around very fast and lift the helicopter straight up into the air.

rotor blade

rotor shaft

tail rotor blade

landing skid

### Stunt plane
A stunt plane can roll, dive, fly in loops, or even upside down!

wing

tail fin

### Microlight
Microlights are very small planes that pilots fly for fun.

fabric wing

propeller

### Passenger airplane
Passenger planes fly people all around the world, on vacation and on business. Have you ever been in a big airplane?

tail fin

### Concorde

The Concorde flies higher and faster than any other passenger airplane.

The Concorde's nose drops down when it takes off or lands so that the pilot can see the runway clearly.

cockpit

wing

The rudder is used to steer the glider.

### Glider

A glider has no engine. It is towed into the sky behind another plane. When the tow cable is released, the glider soars through the air.

### Flying boat

A flying boat has a belly shaped like a boat's hull. It lands on water on this hull. Small floats support the wings.

float

G-BMNU

### Seaplane

A seaplane has floats instead of wheels so that it can take off and land on water.

### Hot-air balloon

This balloon is filled with hot air, which makes it rise up into the sky. Where do you think the passengers ride?

Burners heat the air inside the balloon.

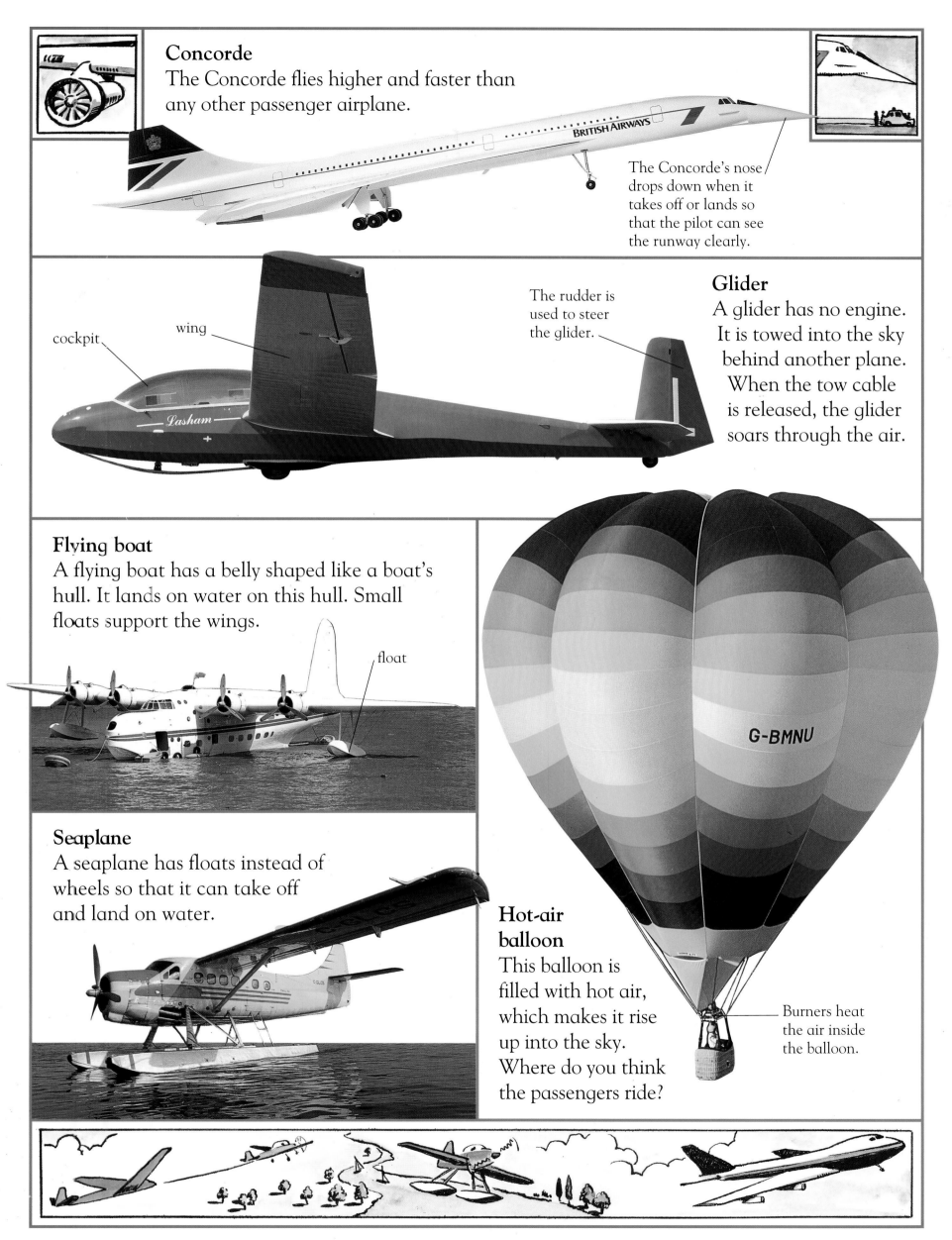

# On the farm

### Tractor
A tractor is a powerful vehicle that pulls other farm machinery. This tractor is pulling a plow to turn over earth and bury any plants.

plow

### Tractor with furrow press
Plowed fields are bumpy. A furrow press flattens the bumps and a power harrow smooths the earth.

power harrow

furrow press

### Tractor with seed drill
This tractor is planting seeds. The seeds drop into the earth and are covered with soil.

cab

This hopper contains the seeds.

cab

tire

### Multipurpose truck
This tough truck is used for lots of different jobs on a farm. It can carry heavy loads and has deep grooves in its tires to keep it from getting stuck in any mud.

### Forage harvester
A forage harvester collects mowed grass and chops it up. The grass is made into a cattle food called silage.

cab

An arm, or boom, supports the shovel.

shovel

## Farm loader

This farm loader is called a Farm Master. It uses its big shovel to carry grain and cattle food around a farm.

## All-terrain vehicle

An all-terrain vehicle, or ATV, can travel over any sort of ground. In Australia, ATVs are often used for rounding up sheep.

## Combine harvester

When grain crops such as wheat, corn, and barley are fully grown, they are cut, or harvested, with a combine harvester.

grain tank

## Rice harvester

A rice harvester is a cutting machine. It chops down rice plants, which are collected from the field later.

## Telescopic handler

Could you lift a bale of hay? It weighs about 44 pounds (20kg). A telescopic handler can lift 64 bales at a time!

Hay bales are lifted on these forks.

19

# At the roadworks

cab

bucket

The legs keep the excavator steady.

688B

Keep clear

## Wheeled excavator
This excavator is like a massive shovel on wheels. Its toothy bucket scoops out deep trenches.

## Grader
A grader has a metal blade that smooths the surface of the earth before a new road is laid.

blade

## Paver
A paver spreads a layer of small stones and warm tar over the flattened earth.

The stones and tar are tipped into this hopper.

blade

## Scraper
A scraper clears a path for a new road by cutting through hills with a sharp blade.

## Compactor
A compactor has spiked wheels that squash down the earth.

blade

exhaust pipe

A canopy protects the driver from sun or rain.

The screed arm lays down the stone and tar mixture.

BARBER-GREENE

BG-250

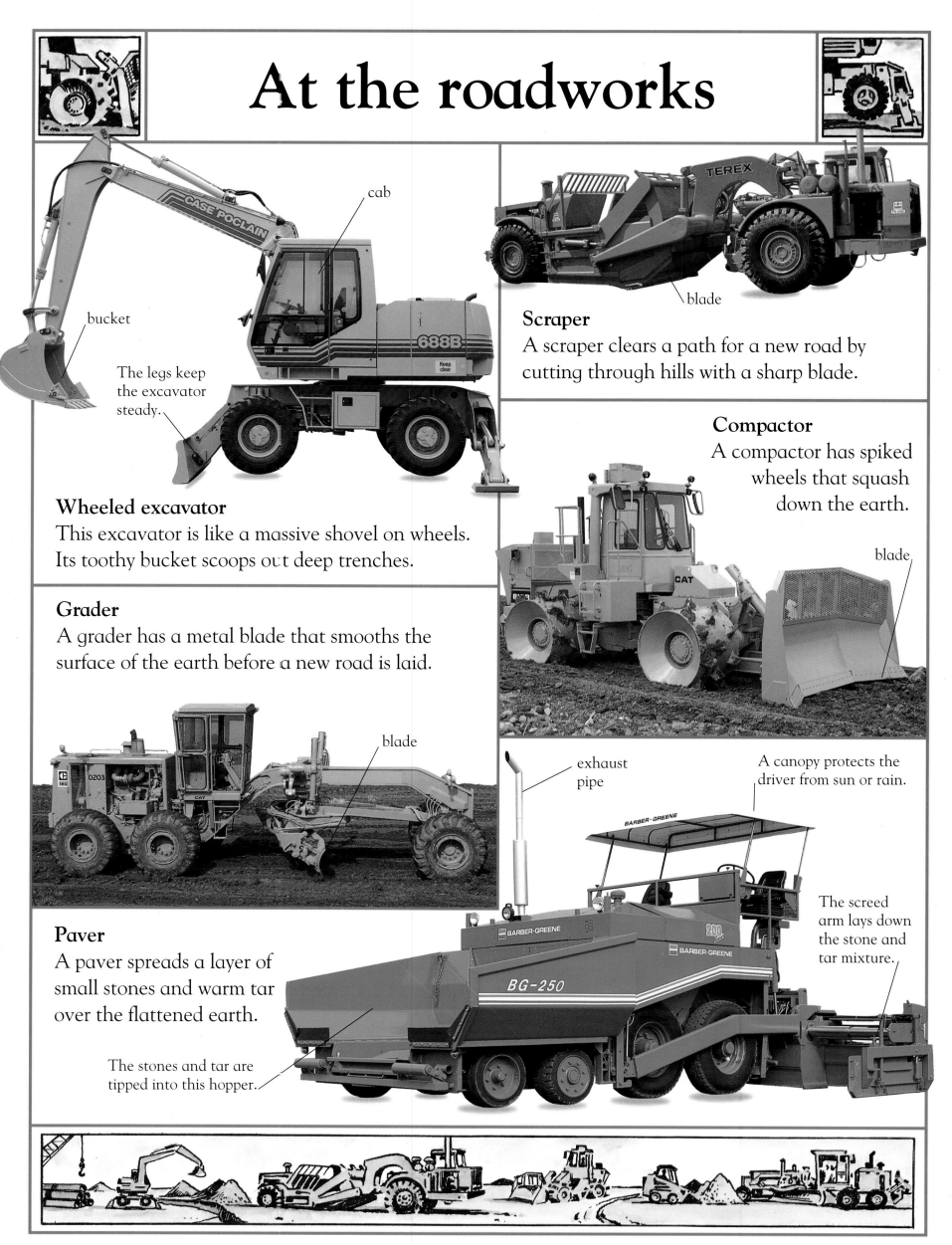

## Chip spreader

A chip spreader drops a thin layer of small stones over the newly laid surface of a road. A roller then presses these into the surface.

## Dump truck

This truck dumps out its heavy load wherever it is needed.

tilting body

## Skid steer

A speedy little skid steer is useful for work where there is not much space.

bucket

headlight

## Telescopic boom

A telescopic boom has a long arm. It helps workers reach high places, such as road lights or bridges.

arm, or boom

wheel

## Roller

A roller uses its massive wheels to flatten the surface of a road.

cab

roller

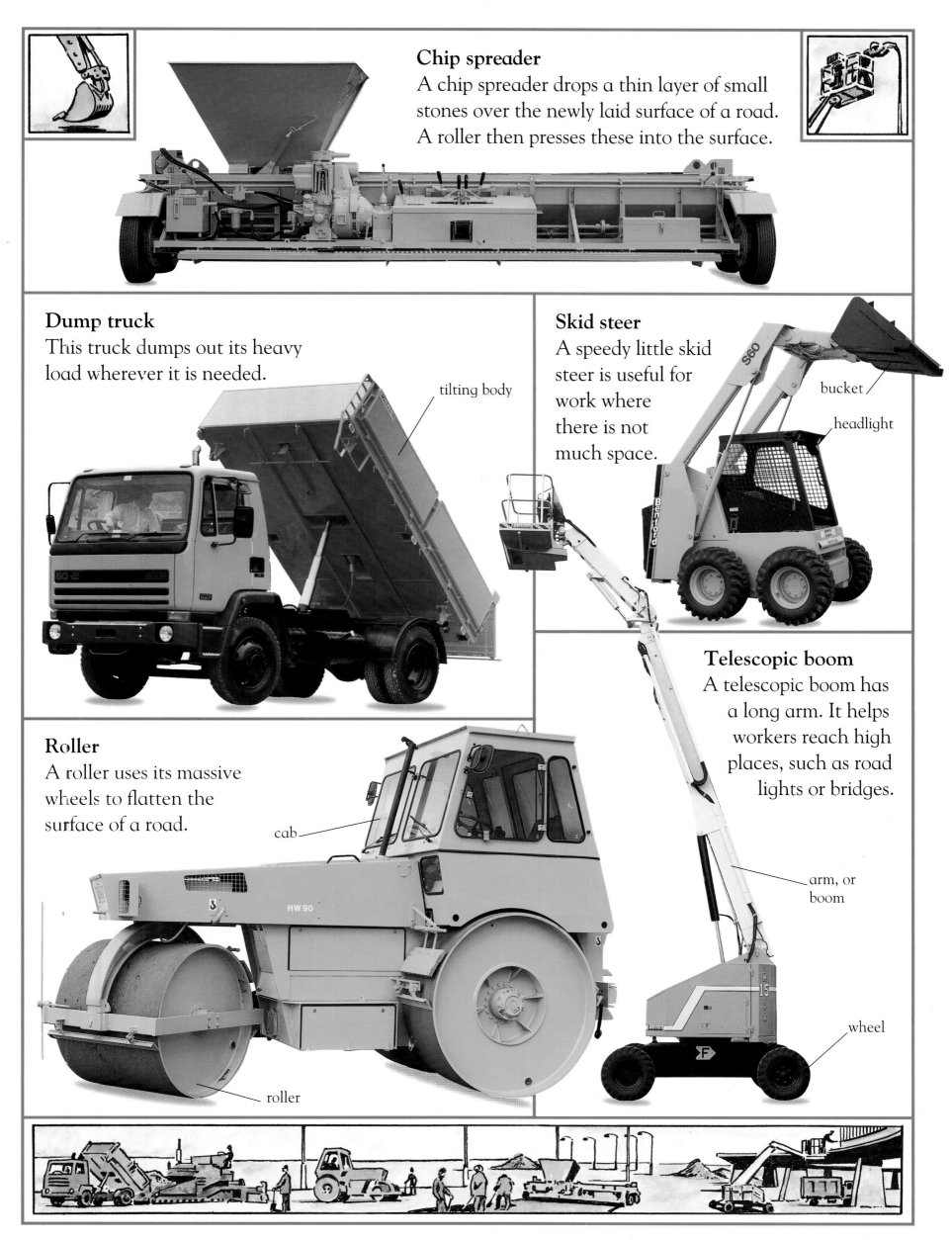

# On the building site

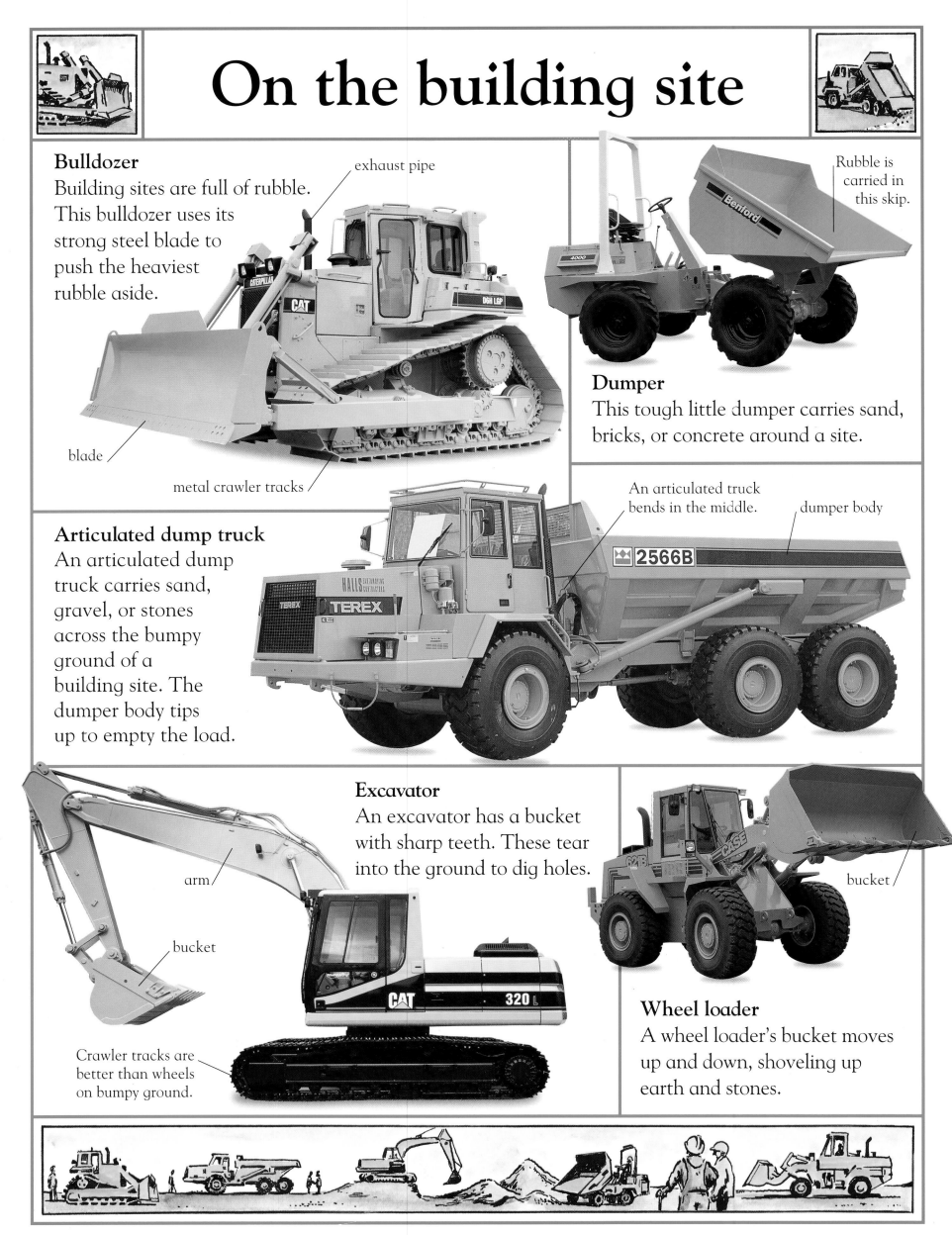

## Bulldozer

Building sites are full of rubble. This bulldozer uses its strong steel blade to push the heaviest rubble aside.

exhaust pipe

blade

metal crawler tracks

Rubble is carried in this skip.

## Dumper

This tough little dumper carries sand, bricks, or concrete around a site.

## Articulated dump truck

An articulated dump truck carries sand, gravel, or stones across the bumpy ground of a building site. The dumper body tips up to empty the load.

An articulated truck bends in the middle.

dumper body

## Excavator

An excavator has a bucket with sharp teeth. These tear into the ground to dig holes.

arm

bucket

Crawler tracks are better than wheels on bumpy ground.

bucket

## Wheel loader

A wheel loader's bucket moves up and down, shoveling up earth and stones.

## Backhoe loader

A backhoe loader can do two different jobs. Can you figure out what it does?

boom

bucket

shovel

## Concrete mixer

A concrete mixer has a big drum that turns around and around to mix concrete. The drum is emptied through a chute.

chute

## Forklift

A forklift is used to move heavy stacks of bricks around a building site.

engine

wheel

## Skip loader

Skips are used as giant garbage bins on building sites. Special trucks collect the skips.

crane arm

truck cab

## Truck loader crane

A truck loader crane has an extending crane arm. On a building site, the crane is used to lift heavy steel bars, called girders, to each new floor of a multi-story building.

# Emergency!

## Police motorcycle

When police need to get around fast, they can use motorcycles to weave through traffic.

## Emergency van

If a car breaks down, an emergency van might be able to help get it moving again.

flashing light

## Ambulance

Ambulances rush people to hospitals. A siren and flashing lights tell other drivers that the ambulance is in a hurry.

## Police boat

In Sydney Harbour, Australia, police use boats to speed across the water to help people in trouble.

POLICE

TELSTAR

## Snowplow

A snowplow has a wide steel blade on the front to shovel snow off the road. It clears the way for cars and trucks.

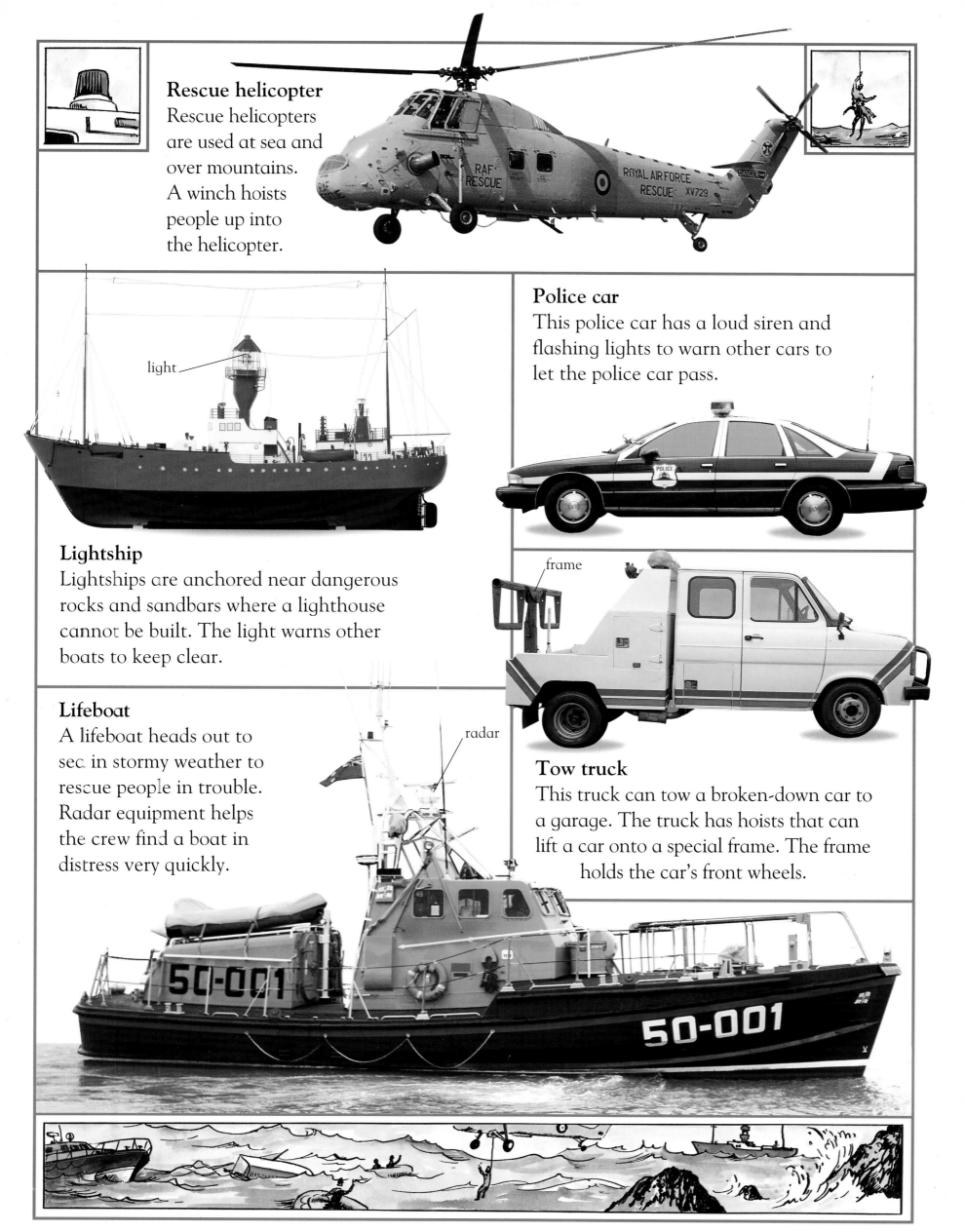

### Rescue helicopter
Rescue helicopters are used at sea and over mountains. A winch hoists people up into the helicopter.

light

### Lightship
Lightships are anchored near dangerous rocks and sandbars where a lighthouse cannot be built. The light warns other boats to keep clear.

### Police car
This police car has a loud siren and flashing lights to warn other cars to let the police car pass.

frame

### Tow truck
This truck can tow a broken-down car to a garage. The truck has hoists that can lift a car onto a special frame. The frame holds the car's front wheels.

### Lifeboat
A lifeboat heads out to sea in stormy weather to rescue people in trouble. Radar equipment helps the crew find a boat in distress very quickly.

radar

50-001

50-001

# Firefighters

## Airport fire engine
An airport fire engine carries huge amounts of water and foam. The water and foam mixture is squirted onto a fire through a monitor.

aerial ladder

monitor

This platform can hold four people.

boom

## Sky-lift engine
A sky-lift engine can hoist a firefighter up to meet the flames of a fire. A water hose runs up the boom, and the firefighter points it at the flames.

## Fire chief's car
This fire car races to the scene of a fire. It arrives with the first fire engines so that the chief fire officer can direct the firemen's efforts and decide if a special rescue truck is needed.

## Fire rescue truck
This truck carries special fire-fighting tools such as radar and chemical-control equipment. It gives extra support to other fire engines.

equipment locker

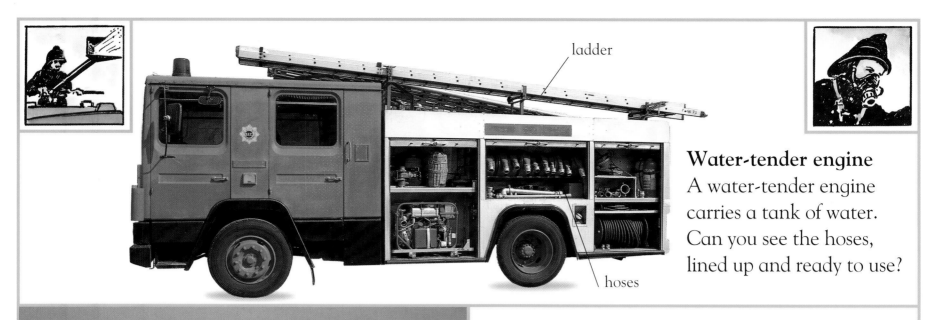

ladder

hoses

## Water-tender engine
A water-tender engine carries a tank of water. Can you see the hoses, lined up and ready to use?

## Rapid intervention vehicle
Rapid intervention vehicles like this one are sometimes used at airports. They can reach a fire faster than a big truck.

## Fire-fighting aircraft
This aircraft has special water tanks that it fills by scooping up water as it skims across the surface of a lake. The water tanks are then emptied over a fire.

monitor

floodlight

3

equipment locker

## Articulated fire truck
This fire truck is articulated, which means that it bends in the middle. This helps it steer over bumpy or muddy ground.

WITTMAN FIELD AIRPORT
WINNEBAGO COUNTY
19

WFA

# At the races

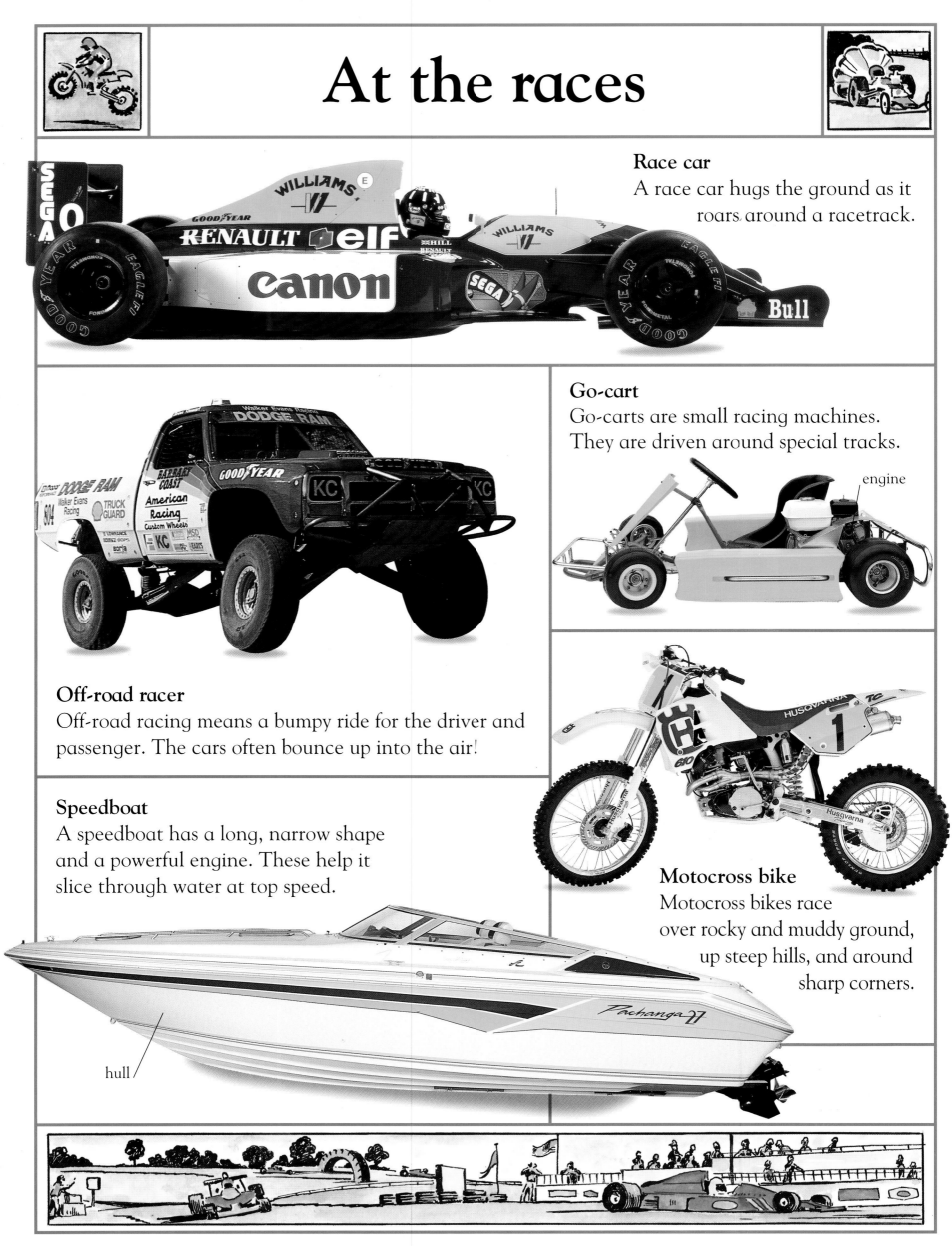

### Race car
A race car hugs the ground as it roars around a racetrack.

### Go-cart
Go-carts are small racing machines. They are driven around special tracks.

engine

### Off-road racer
Off-road racing means a bumpy ride for the driver and passenger. The cars often bounce up into the air!

### Motocross bike
Motocross bikes race over rocky and muddy ground, up steep hills, and around sharp corners.

### Speedboat
A speedboat has a long, narrow shape and a powerful engine. These help it slice through water at top speed.

hull

## Racing motorcycle

This motorcycle races at high speeds on a special track. What differences do you see between this motorcycle and a motocross bike?

## Sidecar racer

A sidecar racer takes two people. They lean from side to side to balance the motorcycle.

## Racing yacht

This racing yacht has a big crew. The crew members have to work hard to make the yacht move as fast as it can. They pull on ropes called sheets to change the position of the sails. The sails catch the wind and make the yacht speed across the water.

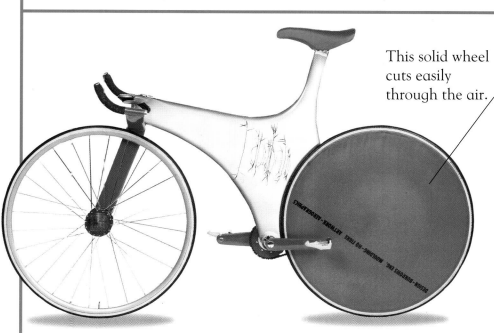

This solid wheel cuts easily through the air.

## Racing bike

This bike is used in races around high-speed cycling tracks. It is very light to help it move fast.

# Amazing machines

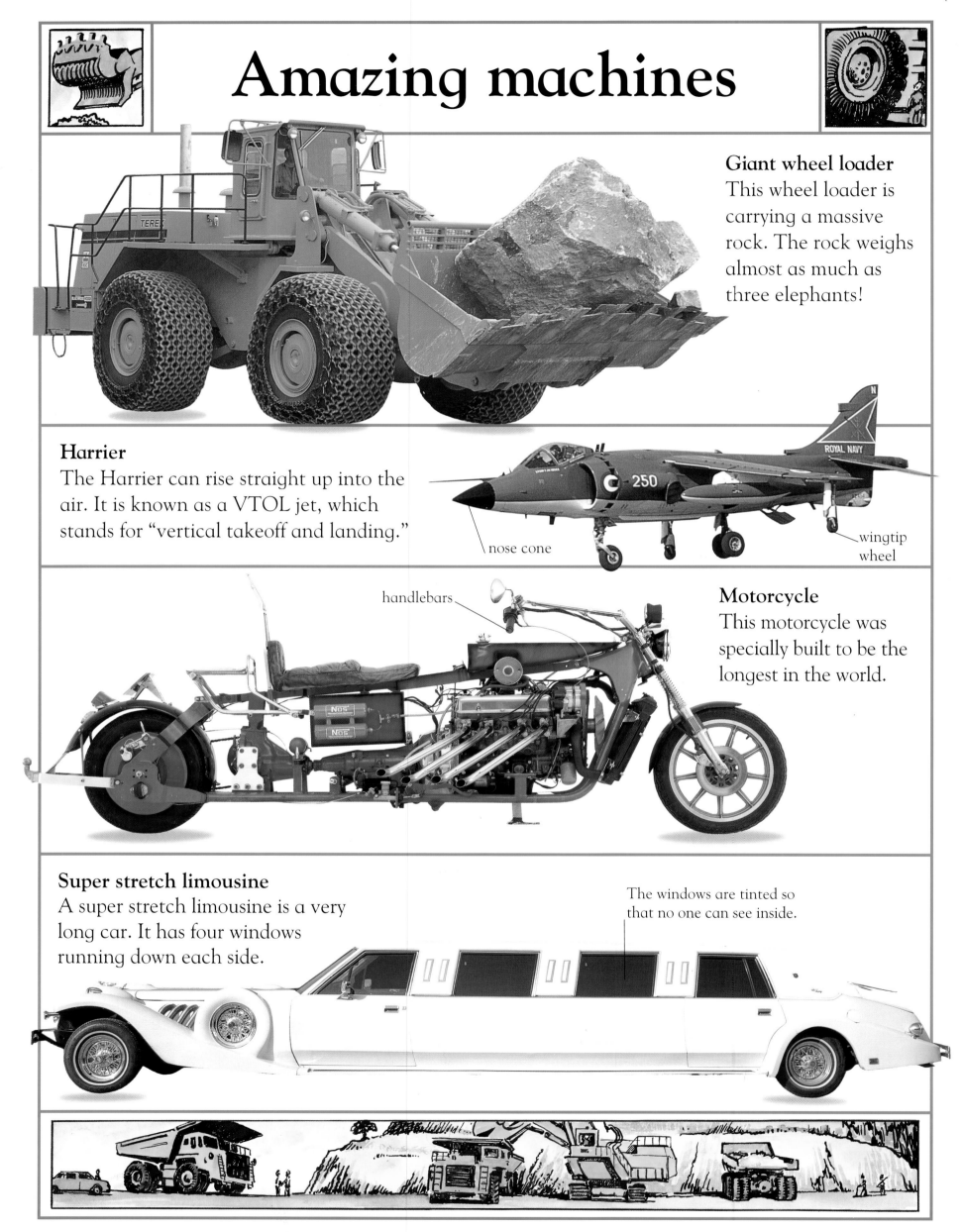

**Giant wheel loader**
This wheel loader is carrying a massive rock. The rock weighs almost as much as three elephants!

**Harrier**
The Harrier can rise straight up into the air. It is known as a VTOL jet, which stands for "vertical takeoff and landing."

nose cone

wingtip wheel

handlebars

**Motorcycle**
This motorcycle was specially built to be the longest in the world.

**Super stretch limousine**
A super stretch limousine is a very long car. It has four windows running down each side.

The windows are tinted so that no one can see inside.

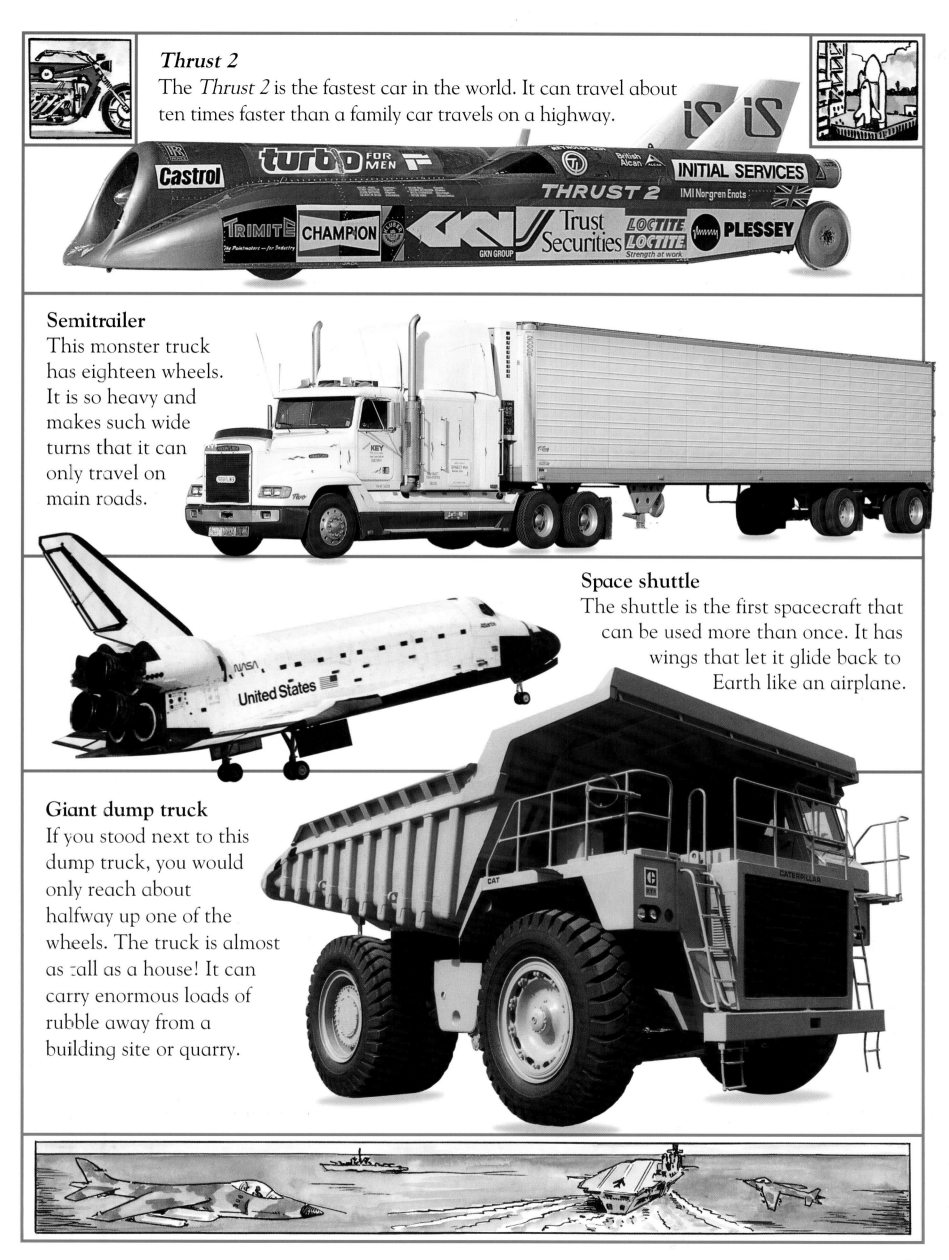

### Thrust 2
The *Thrust 2* is the fastest car in the world. It can travel about ten times faster than a family car travels on a highway.

### Semitrailer
This monster truck has eighteen wheels. It is so heavy and makes such wide turns that it can only travel on main roads.

### Space shuttle
The shuttle is the first spacecraft that can be used more than once. It has wings that let it glide back to Earth like an airplane.

### Giant dump truck
If you stood next to this dump truck, you would only reach about halfway up one of the wheels. The truck is almost as tall as a house! It can carry enormous loads of rubble away from a building site or quarry.

# Index

Airport fire engine . . . 26
all-terrain vehicle . . . 19
ambulance . . . 24
articulated dump truck . . . 22
articulated fire truck . . . 27

Backhoe loader . . . 23
bicycle . . . 8
breakdown train . . . 11
bulldozer . . . 22
bus . . . 8

Cabin cruiser . . . 14
camper van . . . 6
car carrier . . . 6
catamaran . . . 12
Chinese junk . . . 13
chip spreader . . . 21
coach . . . 6
combine harvester . . . 19
compactor . . . 20
Concorde . . . 17
concrete mixer . . . 23
container ship . . . 13
cruise ship . . . 15

Delivery van . . . 8
diesel locomotive . . . 10
dumper . . . 22
dump truck . . . 21

Emergency van . . . 24
excavator
        track . . . 22
        wheeled . . . 20

Farm loader . . . 19
ferry . . . 13
fire chief's car . . . 26
fire-fighting aircraft . . . 27
fire rescue truck . . . 26
fishing trawler . . . 13
flying boat . . . 17
forage harvester . . . 18
forklift . . . 23

Garbage truck . . . 8
giant dump truck . . . 31
giant wheel loader . . . 30
glider . . . 17
go-cart . . . 28
gondola . . . 15
grader . . . 20

Harrier . . . 30
hatchback . . . 8
helicopter . . . 16
high-speed train . . . 11
hot-air balloon . . . 17
hovercraft . . . 13

Inflatable dinghy . . . 15

Jet ski . . . 14

Lifeboat . . . 25
light aircraft . . . 16
lightship . . . 25

Microlight . . . 16
monorail . . . 10
motocross bike . . . 28
motorcycle . . . 6, 30
moving van . . . 9
multipurpose truck . . . 18

Off-road racer . . . 28
outrigger . . . 12

Paddle steamer . . . 14
passenger airplane . . . 16
paver . . . 20
pickup truck . . . 7
police boat . . . 24
police car . . . 25
police motorcycle . . . 24

Race car . . . 28
racing bike . . . 29
racing motorcycle . . . 29
racing yacht . . . 29
rack-and-pinion train . . . 11
rapid intervention vehicle . . . 27
rescue helicopter . . . 25
rice harvester . . . 19
rickshaw . . . 9
roller . . . 21

Sailboat . . . 14
scraper . . . 20
seaplane . . . 17
sedan . . . 7
semitrailer . . . 31
shipping truck . . . 7
shunter . . . 11
sidecar racer . . . 29
skid steer . . . 21
skip loader . . . 23
sky-lift engine . . . 26
snowplow . . . 24
snowplow train . . . 10
space shuttle . . . 31
speedboat . . . 28
sports car . . . 6
station wagon . . . 7
steam train . . . 10
streetcar . . . 10
street sweeper . . . 9
stretch limousine . . . 9
stunt plane . . . 16
submersible . . . 12

subway train . . . 11
super stretch limousine . . . 30

Tanker . . . 7
taxi . . . 9
telescopic boom . . . 21
telescopic handler . . . 19
three-masted ship . . . 15
Thrust 2 . . . 31
tow truck . . . 25
track excavator . . . 22
tractor . . . 18
        with furrow press . . . 18
        with seed drill . . . 18
truck loader crane . . . 23
tug . . . 12

Water-tender engine . . . 27
wheel loader . . . 22
wheeled excavator . . . 20

## Acknowledgments

Dorling Kindersley would like to thank:
Action Vehicles at Shepperton Studios, Middlesex; AirBourne
Aviation at Popham Airfield, Nr Basingstoke; Benford Ltd,
Warwick; Brands Hatch; Case International; Caterpillar Inc.;
G P Edwards; Fairoaks Airport Ltd; FLS Aerospace at London
Stansted Airport; Gilmar Motor Engineers; Mark Goss; Griffiths
Tucker, Liss, Hampshire; Hoverspeed, Dover; JCB; Johnston
Engineering Ltd, Dorking, Surrey; Red Watch at Lambeth Fire
Station, London; Lasham Gliding, Alton, Hampshire; John
McCluskey; New Holland Ford Ltd; P.J.S. (Agricultural
Services) Ltd, Newbury; Harbour Manager's Office at the Port
of Dover; S.E.C. Fire Protection Ltd at Shepperton Studios;
White Watch at Soho Fire Station, London; Blue and Green
Watch at London Stansted Airport Fire Service; Ian Vickerstaff
at Terex Equipment Ltd, Motherwell, Scotland.

Picture credits
t=top, b=bottom, c=center, l=left, r=right, ca=center
above, cb=center below, cra=center right above, crb=center
right below, cla=center left above, clb=center left below

The Aviation Picture Library/Austin J. Brown 27cl; Balloon
Base (Bristol - UK) 5cra, 17br; Pete Biro 28cl; The J. Allan
Cash Photolibrary 17clb, 17bl, 24cr; Caterpillar Inc. 20cr, 20cl;
Edbro plc, Bolton 21cl and cover; First Waste, Hendon, London
8br; Robert Harding Picture Library 14cl/Ian Griffiths:
10br/Adam Woolfit: 9crb; The Image Bank 10cl and cover,
12cl; London Underground Ltd 11tl; David MacKrill
Engineering Group Ltd 23cr; NASA 31clb; National Motor
Museum, Beaulieu 31t; Oshkosh Truck Corporation 27b;
Quadrant 24b, 25t; Guy Ryecart 28t; Tony Stone
Images/Alastair Black: 15t/Michael McQueen: 15b; Tadano-
Faun 4tl, 23b; Terex Equipment Ltd 20tr, 30tl; Zefa 10bl, 11tr,
12cr/Bob Croxford: 30cra/Orion Press: 19bl.

Every effort has been made to trace the copyright holders.
Dorling Kindersley apologizes for any unintentional omissions
and would be pleased, in such cases, to add an
acknowledgment in future editions.